DK READERS

Level 3

Spacebusters: The Race to the Moon
Beastly Tales
Shark Attack!
Titanic
Invaders from Outer Space
Movie Magic
Plants Bite Back!
Time Traveler
Bermuda Triangle
Tiger Tales
Aladdin
Heidi
Zeppelin: The Age of the Airship
Spies
Terror on the Amazon
Disasters at Sea
The Story of Anne Frank
Abraham Lincoln: Lawyer, Leader, Legend
George Washington: Soldier, Hero, President
Extreme Sports
Spiders' Secrets

The Big Dinosaur Dig
Space Heroes: Amazing Astronauts
The Story of Chocolate
School Days Around the World
Polar Bear Alert!
NFL: Whiz Kid Quarterbacks
MLB: Home Run Heroes: Big Mac, Sammy,
    and Junior
MLB: World Series Heroes
MLB: Record Breakers
MLB: Down to the Wire: Baseball's Great
    Pennant Races
Star Wars: Star Pilot
Star Wars: I want to be a Jedi
The X-Men School
Abraham Lincoln: Abogado, Líder, Leyenda
    en español
Al Espacio: La Carrera a la Luna
    en español
*Fantastic Four: The World's Greatest
    Superteam*

Level 4

Days of the Knights
    Volcanoes and Other Natural Disasters
Secrets of the Mummies
    Pirates! Raiders of the High Seas
    Horse Heroes
    Trojan Horse
    Micro Monsters
    Going for Gold!
    Extreme Machines
    Flying Ace: The Story of Amelia Earhart
    Robin Hood
    Black Beauty
    Free at Last! The Story of
        Martin Luther King, Jr.
    Joan of Arc
    Spooky Spinechillers
    Welcome to The Globe! The
        Story of Shakespeare's Theater
Antarctic Adventure
Space Station: Accident on Mir
Atlantis: The Lost City?
Dinosaur Detectives
Danger on the Mountain: Scaling
    the World's Highest Peaks
Crime Busters
The Story of Muhammad Ali
First Flight: The Story of the
    Wright Brothers
D-Day Landings: the Story of
    the Allied Invasion
Solo Sailing
    NFL: NFL's Greatest Upsets
    NFL: Rumbling Running Backs
NFL: Super Bowl!

MLB: Strikeout Kings
MLB: Super Shortstops: Jeter,
    Nomar, and A-Rod
MLB: The Story of the New York Yankees
MLB: The World of Baseball
MLB: October Magic: All the Best
    World Series!
WCW: Feel the Sting
WCW: Going for Goldberg
JLA: Batman's Guide to Crime
    and Detection
JLA: Superman's Guide to the Universe
JLA: Aquaman's Guide to the Oceans
JLA: Wonder Woman's Book of Myths
JLA: Flash's Guide to Speed
JLA: Green Lantern's Guide to
    Great Inventions
The Story of the X-Men: How it all
Began
Creating the X-Men: How Comic
    Books Come to Life
Spider-Man's Amazing Powers
    The Story of Spider-Man
    The Incredible Hulk's Book of Strength
    The Story of the Incredible Hulk
    Transformers: The Awakening
    Transformers: The Quest
Transformers: The Unicron Battles
Transformers: The Uprising
Transformers: Megatron Returns
Transformers: Terracon Attack
Star Wars: Galactic Crisis!
Fantastic Four: Evil Adversaries
Dinosaurs! Battle of the Bones

A Note to Parents

DK READERS is a compelling program for beginning readers, designed in conjunction with leading literacy experts, including Dr. Linda Gambrell, Professor of Education at Clemson University. Dr. Gambrell has served as President of the National Reading Conference, the College Reading Association, and the International Reading Association.

Beautiful illustrations and superb full-color photographs combine with engaging, easy-to-read stories and informational texts to offer a fresh approach to each subject in the series. Each DK READER is guaranteed to capture a child's interest while developing his or her reading skills, general knowledge, and love of reading.

The five levels of DK READERS are aimed at different reading abilities, enabling you to choose the books that are exactly right for your child:

Pre-level 1: Learning to read
Level 1: Beginning to read
Level 2: Beginning to read alone
Level 3: Reading alone
Level 4: Proficient readers

The "normal" age at which a child begins to read can be anywhere from three to eight years old. Adult participation through the lower levels is very helpful for providing encouragement, discussing storylines, and sounding out unfamiliar words.

No matter which level you select, you can be sure that you are helping your child learn to read, then read to learn!

LONDON, NEW YORK,
MELBOURNE, MUNICH, AND DELHI

For DK/BradyGames
Global Strategy Guide Publisher
Mike Degler
Digital and Trade Category Publisher
Brian Saliba
Editor-In-Chief
H. Leigh Davis
Operations Manager
Stacey Beheler
Title Manager
Tim Fitzpatrick
Book Designer
Tim Amrhein
Production Designer
Tracy Wehmeyer

For DK Publishing
Publishing Director
Beth Sutinis
Licensing Editor
Nancy Ellwood
Reading Consultant
Linda B. Gambrell, Ph.D.

For WWE
Director, Home Entertainment & Books
Dean Miller
Photo Department
Frank Vitucci, Joshua Tottenham,
Jamie Nelsen
Copy Editor Kevin Caldwell
Legal Lauren Dienes-Middlen

DK/BradyGAMES
800 East 96th St., 3rd floor
Indianapolis, IN 46240

11 12 13 10 11 10 9 8 7 6 5 4 3 2 1

A catalog record for this book is available from the Library of Congress.

ISBN: 978-0-7566-7608-7 (Paperback)

ISBN: 978-0-7566-8703-8 (Hardback)

Printed and bound by Lake Book

The publisher would like to thank the following for their kind
permission to reproduce their photographs:
All photos courtesy WWE Entertainment, Inc.
All other images © Dorling Kindersley
For further information see: www.dkimages.com

Discover more at
www.dk.com

Contents

DK READERS

READING
3
ALONE

Kofi Kingston®

Written by Kevin Sullivan

DK

DK Publishing

3

Trouble in Paradise

Kofi Kingston is from Ghana, West Africa. However, before he came to WWE, the exciting Superstar spent much of his time on the Caribbean island of Jamaica. Kingston loved the sandy beaches and peaceful blue waters. To him, there was no place in the world more beautiful.

Sometimes bullies walked up and down the island's beaches. They would knock over kids' sandcastles and toss their garbage in the water. This angered Kingston, who refused to stand by and let the bullies ruin the beautiful island. Whenever he saw trouble in paradise, Kingston would confront the bullies and put them in their place.

Kofi Kingston's Stats
- **Height:** 6' (1.83 m)
- **Weight:** 221 lbs. (100 kg)
- **From:** Ghana, West Africa
- **Signature Moves:** Trouble in Paradise, Boom Drop, S.O.S.

A Rising Star

As he patrolled paradise, Kofi
Kingston dreamed of one day becoming a
WWE Superstar. His dream finally came
true when he made his ECW debut on
January 22, 2008. He defeated David
Owen that night and went unbeaten for
the next four months. Along the way, he
beat such Superstars as Santino Marella,
Mike Knox, and Elijah Burke.

Kingston's first big challenge was Shelton Benjamin. Known as the "Gold Standard," Benjamin was considered one of ECW's toughest Superstars. However, Kingston wasn't scared off by the former Intercontinental Champion's reputation. Instead, he stepped into the ring confident that his skills could carry him to victory over Benjamin. Kingston was right; his great in-ring ability led him to two straight wins over the "Gold Standard." The entire WWE Universe immediately took notice of the newcomer. It was clear that Kofi Kingston was a rising star.

Monday Night's Bright Lights

The rivalry between Kofi Kingston and Shelton Benjamin continued for a few more months.

Each Superstar picked up wins over
the other until Kingston finally ended
their bitter grudge with a big victory over
the "Gold Standard" in an Extreme Rules
Match in June 2008. After proving his
superiority over Benjamin, it was clear
that Kingston was ready for bigger and
better challenges. He was ready for the
bright lights of *Monday Night Raw*.

Kingston was drafted to *Raw* in late June 2008. Moving to Monday nights meant that he would compete against WWE's very best, including John Cena, Edge, and Shawn Michaels. Some fans feared Kingston would get lost in the shuffle. However, unlike many Superstars before him, the move to WWE's main stage didn't intimidate Kingston. In fact, he made a huge impact just after being drafted.

At the *Night of Champions* pay-per-view, the *Raw* newcomer hit Chris Jericho with his Trouble in Paradise signature move to win the Intercontinental Championship. It was Kingston's first-ever title victory.

Kingston's win at *Night of Champions* shocked many, especially Jericho. Nevertheless, the fans that followed the young Superstar's career from the very beginning weren't surprised. They knew his unique style of high-flying offense would one day take him to the top of WWE.

Kofi Kingston's Signature Moves

Trouble in Paradise (leaping corkscrew roundhouse kick): With his groggy opponent standing in front of him, Kingston jumps into the air, twists his body completely around, and lands a kick to his adversary's head.

Boom Drop (jumping double leg drop): With his opponent down on the mat, Kingston runs off the ropes, jumps into the air, and drops both of his legs on top of his foe.

S.O.S.: Kingston grabs his opponent at the side. He then flips himself forward while sweeping his rival's leg. The fast sweeping motion results in Kingston's opponent landing on his back.

Winner Take All

Kofi Kingston proudly defended his newly won Intercontinental Championship against all comers. Many tried, but nobody on the *Raw* roster could defeat the champ for the gold. Then Kingston agreed to team up with Women's Champion Mickie James to defend his title against Santino Marella and Beth Phoenix in a Winner Take All Tag Team Match at *SummerSlam*.

This decision proved to be the beginning of the end for Kingston's Intercontinental Championship reign. During the match, Beth used her power advantage over Mickie to pick up the win for her team. Because of the contest's unique rules, Beth's win meant Kingston lost his title to Marella without even being involved in the deciding pin.

Straight to the Top

Although Kofi Kingston lost his Intercontinental Championship at *SummerSlam*, his career began to reach new heights in the fall of 2008. His infectious smile and high-flying style of offense made him one of *Raw*'s most popular Superstars. With the fans firmly behind him, it wasn't long before Kingston found himself competing alongside many of WWE's top main-eventers, including CM Punk.

At *Unforgiven* in September 2008,
Kingston attempted to save Punk from a
backstage attack by Randy Orton, Ted
DiBiase, Cody Rhodes, and Manu.
Unfortunately, Kingston's efforts did
little to stop the brutal assault.
However, it did mark the beginning of a
very successful partnership between CM
Punk and Kingston.

The new team of Punk and Kingston finally gained revenge from their attackers when they beat DiBiase and Rhodes for the World Tag Team Championship on October 27, 2008. They held the title for six weeks before The Miz and John Morrison defeated them at a non-televised live event in Hamilton, Ontario, Canada.

Controlled Frenzy

At just 221 pounds (100 kg), Kofi Kingston is one of WWE's smaller Superstars. Men like Big Show, Mark Henry, and The Great

Khali outweigh him by several hundred pounds. Kingston doesn't let his size hold him back. Instead, he uses his lighter frame to his advantage by quickly bouncing around the ring in ways that larger Superstars cannot. This unique style is known as the "controlled frenzy" of Kofi Kingston.

The high-flying Superstar displayed his "controlled frenzy" in a Money in the Bank Ladder Match at the 25th Anniversary of *WrestleMania*. In the end, CM Punk walked away with the win, but Kingston's offense was so impressive that the WWE Universe is still talking about it years later.

What is a Money in the Bank Ladder Match?

A briefcase holding a contract for a World Championship Match hangs from the arena ceiling, while several Superstars battle in the ring below. The competitors use ladders in an attempt to reach the briefcase. The first Superstar to grab the briefcase is the winner and receives a World Championship Match any time he wants.

United States Champion

Kofi Kingston added more gold to his trophy case when he defeated Montel Vontavious Porter for the United States Championship in June 2009. Just as he did when he was the Intercontinental Champion, Kingston proudly defended his title against all comers, including the monstrous Big Show.

Three months after winning the U.S. Championship, Kingston teamed with Primo to take on The Miz and Jack Swagger. During the match, The Miz stole Kingston's title from ringside and ran off. Luckily, the champ was

able to get his gold back the next week, but he had it only briefly before The Miz stole it yet again.

The situation became even more confusing for Kingston when Swagger jumped in and stole the gold from The Miz.

Kingston thought he finally put all the craziness behind him when he beat both The Miz and Swagger at a pay-per-view event in October.

However, the next night on *Raw*, guest host Ben Roethlisberger demanded he put the U.S. Championship on the line one more time, this time against The Miz in one-on-one action.

Kingston was unable to fend off The Miz on this night and lost the title after an impressive four-month reign.

Kofi Kingston's Title History

Intercontinental Championship:
June 29, 2008 – August 17, 2008

World Tag Team Championship:
October 27, 2008 – December 13, 2008

United States Championship:
June 1, 2009 – October 5, 2009

Intercontinental Championship:
May 23, 2010 – August 6, 2010

Sole Survivor

Kofi Kingston interfered in the John Cena-versus-Randy Orton WWE Championship Match at *Bragging Rights* 2009. In the end, The Viper lost the match and blamed the defeat on

Kingston. This set up the biggest rivalry of Kingston's young career. For the next several weeks, Orton continually tried to gain revenge, but Kingston managed to stay one step ahead of The Viper. Kingston even proved his greatness at *Survivor Series*, where he captained a squad of Superstars to victory over Team Orton.

In fact, of the ten Superstars included in the match, Kingston was the only one left standing at the end.

The grudge between Kingston and Orton continued for the next few months, with each Superstar picking up wins along the way. By 2010, the thrilling rivalry had come to an end, but Kingston's time as an elite Superstar was just beginning.

Survivor Series 2009:
Team Kingston vs. Team Orton

Team Kingston: Mark Henry, R-Truth, Montel Vontavious Porter, Christian, and Kofi Kingston

Team Orton: Cody Rhodes, Ted DiBiase, CM Punk, William Regal, and Randy Orton

Climbing the Ladder

One year after amazing the WWE Universe with his "controlled frenzy" during the annual Money in the Bank Ladder Match, Kofi Kingston was at it again at *WrestleMania XXVI* in Arizona. While the victory ultimately went to Jack Swagger, fans will forever remember Kingston using two ends of a broken ladder as stilts.

Never before had anybody been so innovative in the ring. For Kingston, this *WrestleMania* moment will live forever on WWE highlight reels.

Kofi Kingston's Money in the Bank Ladder Matches

WrestleMania XXV: Kofi Kingston vs. Christian vs. Finlay vs. Shelton Benjamin vs. Kane vs. Montel Vontavious Porter vs. Mark Henry vs. CM Punk (winner)

WrestleMania XXVI: Kofi Kingston vs. Evan Bourne vs. Shelton Benjamin vs. Christian vs. Kane vs. Matt Hardy vs. Drew McIntyre vs. Dolph Ziggler vs. Montel Vontavious Porter vs. Jack Swagger (winner)

Money in the Bank: Kofi Kingston vs. Big Show vs. Christian vs. Matt Hardy vs. Cody Rhodes vs. Drew McIntyre vs. Dolph Ziggler vs. Kane (winner)

Making a Move

Kofi Kingston's time on *Raw* came to a sudden stop when he was drafted to *SmackDown* in April 2010. The change in scenery did little to slow the young Superstar. In a moment very similar to his *Raw* debut, Kingston beat Chris Jericho in his first *SmackDown* match. The win was the perfect jumpstart for Kingston, who then went on to defeat Christian in a tournament to crown a new Intercontinental Champion. However, there was just one problem: the previous champion, Drew McIntyre, had a note from Mr. McMahon. In the note, the WWE Chairman wrote that McIntyre was still the Intercontinental Champion.

Thanks to Mr. McMahon's note, Kingston was forced to give the Intercontinental Championship back to the "Chosen One." *SmackDown* fans screamed out in anger over the injustice, but Kingston refused to pout. Instead, he focused all of his attention on gaining revenge from McIntyre.

Kingston's chance at payback came when he challenged McIntyre for the Intercontinental Championship at *Over the Limit* 2010.

Using Mr. McMahon's note as motivation, the *SmackDown* newcomer dominated much of the match. Kingston finally put the "Chosen One" out of his misery when he hit the S.O.S. for the win and the gold. After the match, McIntyre demanded that *SmackDown* General Manager Theodore Long reverse the decision, but that never happened. This time, there was no returning the title to the "Chosen One." Kofi Kingston was the official Intercontinental Champion.

Double Duty

Kofi Kingston spent the next several months pulling double duty. Not only did he defend his Intercontinental Championship each week on *SmackDown*, but he also served as a "Pro" on Season 2 of *NXT*.

As an *NXT* Pro, Kingston was responsible for mentoring the career of rookie Michael McGillicutty. Under Kingston's guidance, McGillicutty developed the necessary skills to become a true WWE Superstar. The impressive rookie used these new abilities to outlast many *NXT* rookies, including Alex Riley and Husky Harris.

After Season 2 of *NXT* ended, McGillicutty used the knowledge he learned from Kingston to impress Wade Barrett. McGillicutty's skills so impressed the Nexus leader that he soon welcomed the rookie into his successful group of Superstars.

What is NXT?

NXT is a television show that pairs up WWE Superstars (or Pros), such as Kofi Kingston, with aspiring competitors (or Rookies), like Michael McGillicutty. Each week, the Pros mentor the Rookies in matches and challenges. During the season, the WWE Universe, along with the Pros, vote on which Rookies they like the best. The Rookies with the fewest votes are eliminated along the way. A winner is finally announced at the season finale. The grand prize is a WWE contract and a championship match.

Zig Zagged

Despite the pressures of being an *NXT* Pro, Kofi Kingston successfully defended his Intercontinental

Championship throughout much of the process. However, in August 2010, outside interference by Official *SmackDown* Consultant Vickie Guerrero finally proved too much for the champ to handle. As a result, Kingston lost his title to the smug Dolph Ziggler on an episode of *SmackDown*.

Afterward, Kingston set out to prove that he was a better competitor than Ziggler despite losing the gold around his waist.

Over the next several weeks, Kingston accomplished this goal by defeating the new champ two different times. But the wins came by disqualification and countout, which meant the title could not change hands.

SmackDown General Manager Theodore Long noticed that Ziggler was purposely losing by disqualification and countout so that he would not lose his title. At *Night of Champions* 2010, Long demanded Ziggler defend his title against Kingston once again. This time, even if Ziggler lost by disqualification or countout, he would lose the Intercontinental Championship to Kingston.

Heading into the match, nearly the entire WWE Universe assumed Kingston would win the title. Ziggler's girlfriend, Vickie, had other ideas. The devious consultant's presence at ringside was distraction enough for Kingston to lose his focus and fall victim to a Zig Zag from the Intercontinental Champion.

A Bright Future

The loss at *Night of Champions* failed to set Kofi Kingston back for long. He quickly rebounded with wins over top Superstars such as Jack Swagger and Drew McIntyre.

The victories proved that it's nearly impossible to keep a good man like Kingston down for long. With his "controlled frenzy" style of offense and charismatic personality, there is no doubt the exciting young Superstar will be amazing the WWE Universe for many years to come.

Glossary

Adversary
Opponent, challenger, enemy

Brutal
Harsh, vicious, cruel

Charismatic
Charming, appealing, likable

Consultant
Advisor, expert, mentor

Continually
Repeatedly, without stopping

Debut
Someone's or something's first appearance

Disqualification
Ban, exclusion

Distraction
Interference, disturbance, interruption

Dominate
Control, rule, overwhelm

Drafted
Invited, called into service, recruited, enrolled

Eliminated
Removed, abolished, rejected

Finale
Big finish, climax, ending

Frenzy
Burst of activity, uncontrolled behavior

Groggy
Unsteady, wobbly, dizzy, dazed

Grudge
Lasting bitterness, resentment, or ill will

Highlight
The most exciting, memorable, or important part of something

Impressive
Remarkable, inspiring, memorable

Infectious
Contagious, capable of being passed from one person to another

Injustice
Unfairness, mistreatment of someone or something

Innovative
New and creative, inventive

Interfere
Hinder, disturb, obstruct

Intimidate
Frighten, scare, bully, threaten

Jumpstart
Trigger, beginning, spark

Mentoring
Teaching, instructing, training

Motivation
Inspiration, purpose, enthusiasm

Paradise
A place or condition of perfect happiness

Patrol
Guard, watch

Pay-per-view
A television program that viewers can watch for a fee

Rebounded
Recovered, bounced back, returned

Rivalry
A heightened sense of competitiveness between opponents

Rookie
Novice, beginner, amateur, apprentice

Signature move
In WWE, a special technique or tactic that is closely associated with a Superstar

Superiority
The state of being better than something or someone else

Tournament
An event or competition made up of a series of games, rounds, or contests

Ultimately
Eventually, finally, at last

Unique
Special, one of a kind

Index